A World of Festivals

Party Time

Jean Coppendale

Chrysalis Children's Books

First published in the UK in 2003 by
ⓔ Chrysalis Children's Books
The Chrysalis Building, Bramley Road, London W10 6SP

ISBN 184138 8440

British Library Cataloguing in Publication Data for this book is available from the British Library.

A Belitha Book
Editorial Manager: Joyce Bentley
Assistant Editor: Clare Chambers

Produced by
Tall Tree Ltd
Editor: Jon Richards
Consultant: Stephanie Batley
Picture Researcher: Dan Brooks
Artwork: Piers Harper

Printed in China

10 9 8 7 6 5 4 3 2 1

Picture Credits
All reasonable efforts have been made to trace the relevant copyright holders of the images contained within this book. If we were unable to reach you, please contact Chrysalis Children's Books.

B = bottom; C = centre; L = left; R = right; T = top.
Corbis – back cover, 12, 15, 16, 26, 27. **Eye Ubiquitous** – front cover, 1, 4, 7, 8, 9, 17, 18, 19, 21, 22. **Paul Nightingale** – front cover br, 13, 14, 20. **Spectrum Colour Library** – 5, 6, 10, 11, 23, 24, 25.

Contents

Introduction

Street parties and big, noisy **parades** are an important part of festivals all over the world.

This man is dancing in the Notting Hill Carnival in London.

Festival parties and parades usually include lots of music and dancing.

These men are dressed in traditional costumes for the **Alpine** Festival in Switzerland.

People dress up in all sorts of costumes. Their outfits can be frightening or funny, ugly or beautiful – but they are nearly always bright and colourful.

Street Parties

Colourful parades with dancing and music are a feature of many festivals.

The people in costumes throw oranges to the crowd during the Gilles Parade.

The Gilles Parade

People in the Gilles Parade in Belgium dress in red, yellow and black costumes with tall, feathered hats.

The Notting Hill Carnival begins with a special children's parade.

Notting Hill Carnival

People at the Notting Hill Carnival in London wear amazing costumes and fill the streets. There are also hundreds of **floats** and lots of steel bands and musicians.

FESTIVAL DIARY

Gilles Parade
Belgium
February or March

Notting Hill Carnival
United Kingdom
August

Rio Carnival

Mardi Gras is a time of celebration, with huge, loud parties and carnivals.

Mardi Gras dancers wear bright, colourful costumes.

Feast, then fast

Mardi Gras means 'Fat Tuesday'. This comes from a **Christian** tradition when people feasted and celebrated before the **fasting** period of **Lent**.

There is a prize for the best costume and float in the Mardi Gras Carnival.

Mardi Gras

Rio de Janeiro in Brazil holds a carnival for Mardi Gras every year. The festival includes four days of street parties and parades.

FESTIVAL DIARY

Mardi Gras Carnival
Brazil
February or March

Mask Festival

Festival masks come in many different designs and colours. There is even a festival dedicated to masks.

Many people dress up in beautiful costumes for the Mask Festival.

Masked balls
Every year, the city of Venice, Italy, holds a **Masquerade**, or Mask Festival. People wear masks and go to parties, balls and concerts.

Lots of shops and street stalls in Venice sell masks.

Feathers and sequins
Festival masks can be made from paper, **papier-mâché** or leather. The masks can be decorated with feathers and sequins.

FESTIVAL DIARY

Venice Mask Festival
Italy
February

Food Festivals

Every type of food has its own festival in places all around the world.

During the great tomato battle, thousands of people throw soft tomatoes at each other for up to an hour.

Tomato Festival

La Tomatina Festival in Spain lasts for a week, with street parties and fireworks. The highlight is a great tomato battle in the town square.

People visiting the festival eat about 50 tonnes of chocolate – that's the same as 10 elephants!

Chocolate Festival
Every year in the city of Perugia, Italy, there is a chocolate festival that includes chocolate tasting. The town even has a special chocolate museum.

FESTIVAL DIARY

La Tomatina
Spain
August

Chocolate Festival
Italy
October

Happy Birthday

Birthdays are times when a person can celebrate being one year older.

Each band of coloured wool stands for a year of the child's life.

God's Eyes

In many South American countries, children are given God's Eyes on their birthdays. These are made of two sticks tied together and woven with strands of coloured wool.

A birthday cake has one candle for every year of the person's age.

Presents and parties
In many places around the world, birthdays are celebrated with parties where family and friends give cards and presents.

FESTIVAL FACT
Blowing out the candles on a birthday cake all at once is thought to bring good luck.

15

Being Together

There are many festivals that celebrate the love between two people.

Couples give gifts to each other on their wedding **anniversary**.

Wedding anniversary

A wedding anniversary celebrates the years a couple has been married. It is held every year on the day of the couple's wedding.

During Tanabata, people write wishes on strips of paper, called tanzaku. These are then tied to bamboo branches.

Tanabata
Tanabata, or the Star Festival, in Japan celebrates an old folk story about two lovers who could only meet for one day every year.

FESTIVAL DIARY

Tanabata
Japan
July or August

Gion Festival

The Gion Festival is held in the city of Kyoto, Japan.

Gion floats can be two storeys high.

Generous gift

Gion celebrates a time long ago when Kyoto was saved from a terrible disease. There is a parade of floats to thank the gods for saving the city.

Hoko floats carry musicians who play traditional music on pipes and drums.

Pulling together

There are two types of floats in the parade. Yama are small floats carried on people's shoulders. Hoko are large floats pulled by many people.

FESTIVAL DIARY

Gion
Japan
July

19

Halloween

Halloween is a very old festival. It dates from a time when people believed that ghosts came back to haunt them.

Pumpkins are hollowed out to make jack-o'-lanterns.

Scary faces
To scare the ghosts away, people lit fires or carved ugly faces out of vegetables.

Children wear fancy dress to play trick or treat.

Trick or treat

Children go around to their neighbours' houses calling 'trick or treat!'. The neighbours then give sweets or money to stop the children from playing tricks on them.

FESTIVAL DIARY

Halloween
Christian
31 October

Arts Festivals

During arts festivals, artists and performers come together to celebrate and to entertain.

People at the **Eisteddfod** dress up in Welsh and Celtic costumes.

Eisteddfod
The Eisteddfod is a festival of Welsh music, poetry, singing and dancing. Competitions are held to find the best writers, artists and performers.

During the festival, city streets are filled with performers and face painters.

Edinburgh Festival

The Edinburgh Festival in Scotland is the world's largest arts festival. It celebrates theatre, music, dance, drama, comedy and even the circus.

FESTIVAL DIARY

Eisteddfod
Wales
August

Edinburgh Festival
Scotland
August

Song and Dance

Festivals often involve singing and dancing. They help to get everyone into the party mood.

During the Feria, women and girls dress up in traditional Spanish costume.

Feria
The Feria is held every year in the city of Seville in Spain. The streets are full of music and people perform traditional **flamenco** dances.

There is a competition to find the best player of the traditional Alpine horn at the Alpine Festival.

Alpine Festival
The Alpine Festival is held in Switzerland once every three years. People take part in singing and **yodelling** competitions.

Corpus Christi

Corpus Christi means 'the body of Christ'. This festival is one of the highlights of the year for the Catholic Church.

People collect flowers from the town and cover a whole street with them to make a flower carpet.

Carpet of flowers
The town of Genzano, in Italy, holds a flower festival during Corpus Christi.

These South American dancers are dressed in **Inca** costumes for the Corpus Christi festival.

South America

In some parts of South America, the Corpus Christi festival has been combined with traditional Native American ceremonies.

Try This!

Ask an adult to help you with these activities.

Make some God's Eyes

You will need:

- two short sticks
- strands of different coloured wool
(one for each year of the person's age)
- thread

- coloured beads
- scissors
- PVA glue

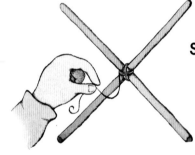

1 Make a cross with the two sticks and wrap some thread around them to tie them together.

2 Put a dab of glue on one end of some wool and stick it onto the centre of the sticks.

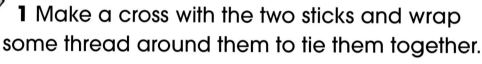

3 Wrap the wool over and under each stick in turn. When you want to change colours, glue the end of the wool around one stick.

4 To start again with a new colour, glue the wool around the same stick and then continue as before, wrapping the wool over and under the sticks.

5 To finish, glue some coloured beads onto the ends of the sticks.

Make a Carnival Mask

You will need:

- strong card
- PVA glue
- paints or felt-tip pens
- plant stick

- scissors
- coloured feathers
- glitter and sequins
- coloured beads

1 Draw the outline of the mask onto the card.

2 Paint or colour your mask and leave it to dry.

3 Ask an adult to cut out the mask shape.

4 Dab glue onto your mask and cover it in glitter, sequins or beads around the eyeholes and stick feathers along the top.

5 Glue a plant stick on one side of your mask so that you can hold it in front of your face.

How to Say...

Corpus Christi
say *cor-pus cris-tee*

Eisteddfod
say *ay-steth-vod*

Gilles
say *jeel*

Gion
say *gee-on*

Halloween
say *ha-lo-ween*

Hoko
say *ho-ko*

Mardi Gras
say *mar-dee gra*

Masquerade
say *mask-er-aid*

Tanabata
say *ta-na-ba-ta*

Tanzaku
say *tan-za-koo*

Tomatina
say *to-ma-tee-na*

Yama
say *ya-ma*

Glossary

Alpine
Something is called Alpine if it comes from the area around the Alps mountains in central Europe.

Anniversary
An event that occurs on the same day each year.

Christian
Someone who believes in Jesus Christ and his teachings.

Eisteddfod
A Welsh arts festival. The word Eisteddfod means 'a session'.

Fasting
A person is fasting when they stop eating food for a period.

Flamenco
A type of dance music from Spain where a singer and musicians accompany a dancer.

Float
A vehicle that carries a band, dancers or a scene in a parade or carnival.

Incas
A group of people from South America. The Incas ruled an empire around the country of Peru over 500 years ago.

Lent
A period celebrated by Christians just before Easter that lasts for 40 days. This period was a time for fasting and prayer.

Masquerade
A party or ball where the guests wear masks to hide their identity.

Papier-mâché
A hard substance made by soaking strips of paper in glue. These strips can be shaped when they are wet and harden as they dry.

Parade
A march or procession of bands, floats, vehicles and people.

Yodelling
A high-pitched singing used to call over long distances in mountain regions.

Index